HARD TIMES IN NATAL
AND
THE WAY OUT

COLIN WEBB

NATAL AND ZULULAND SERIES

Much significant and fascinating published material on manifold aspects of the Natal-Zululand region is not known to researchers, collectors and general readers, because of its rarity or inaccessibility or because it is in an unfamiliar language. The aim of this series is to make select pamphlets, newspaper and journal articles, and pertinent extracts from books more readily available and, occasionally, to provide translations into English.

The name of Colin Webb is inseparable from the historiography of Natal and Zululand. It represents sound scholarship, original, imaginative thinking and a passionate concern for the past of this region in all its diversity. Colin Webb was keenly interested in the University of Natal Press, which published all his books, and drew much of his material from collections held in the Killie Campbell Africana Library. It is appropriate that this joint series on Natal and Zululand should be named for him.

John Laband
Series Editor

R.H. LAMB

HARD TIMES IN NATAL

AND

THE WAY OUT

Introduced by

JOHN LAMBERT

Killie Campbell Africana Library
Durban
University of Natal Press
Pietermaritzburg
1992

This pamphlet has been reset except for the title page, the photograph of Lamb and pages 31–38, which are reproduced in facsimile. In typesetting certain conventions of the period have been observed to retain the character of the original. Editing has been limited to the correction of obvious typographical errors.

ISBN 0 86980 879 6

ISBN 0 86980 872 9 (Set)

This edition is limited to 250 numbered
copies and 26 presentation copies.

This copy is number   145

Typeset in the University of Natal Press, Pietermaritzburg
Printed by Rapid Results College, Durban

INTRODUCTION

Ridgeway Haines Lamb was born in the mid-nineteenth century near Philadelphia in the United States of America. He qualified as a dentist at the Philadelphia Dental College in 1875 and in the following years he travelled the world, making a living both as a dentist and as a writer. He seems to have been particularly fond of the Orient and lived for a while in India where he edited and published the *American Dentist*, and in Ceylon where he edited the *Dental Health Journal*. In 1896 he arrived in Natal for his first visit. He was a flamboyant character and his chequered career suggests that he was an adventurer and perhaps even an opportunist. He was not above boasting of his background and his achievements, yet when the second Anglo-Boer War broke out in 1899 he speedily removed himself from the scene of possible danger. He spent the next few years in the East before returning to the United States in the early twentieth century where he joined the Labadie Lecture and Amusement Bureau in Philadelphia and New York.

Shortly before 1906, he returned to Natal and opened a dental practice in Durban. He seems to have experienced difficulties attracting patients and in 1907 he advertised his practice in two pamphlets which he distributed throughout the colony. The Natal Medical Council found him guilty of disgraceful professional conduct and, at its request, the Governor-in-Council struck him off the Dental Register in October.[1] Although it is not clear whether his decision to write *Hard Times in Natal and the Way Out* resulted from this experience, the virulence of his attacks on colonial officialdom does suggest that he was harbouring a grudge. Within months, in February 1908, *Hard Times* was published, bearing eloquent testimony to his abiding confidence in his qualifications to instruct the settlers of Natal on the nature of their shortcomings and on how they could remedy these deficiencies.

That these deficiencies were manifold cannot be denied. Not only had the colony been plagued with more than a normal share of problems in the years before Lamb wrote his pamphlet, it was also saddled with one of the most incompetent administrations in the British Empire. Compared to the other self-governing British colonies, Natal was underdeveloped and backward. She had a very low per capita income with about 85 per cent of her population living in rural areas.

Of this rural population, the overwhelming majority consisted of African homestead cultivators who, through a number of reasons, had become steadily impoverished during the decades of British rule. By the turn of the century maize was virtually their only cash crop yet few remained in a position where they produced sufficient for their own needs let alone those of the community. Most Africans had been sucked into the migrant labour market. Much of the urban produce market had been captured by Indian market gardeners who were also expanding into rural areas. The white farming sector dominated the best land and agricultural resources in Natal. Yet the average farmer contributed little to the economy. He under-utilized his lands and produced a meagre proportion of the produce consumed in the colony. Agriculture contributed less than 20 per cent of Natal's economic production and virtually all of this percentage was supplied by a small number of well-to-do sugar planters and midland farmers.

The colony's manufacturing sector was also underdeveloped and was involved with little other than the processing of agricultural products. A list of industries would include few that could not be found in an English county town and, as late as 1914, the gross value of their output was less than £10 million a year.[2]

The slow development of Natal's agricultural and manufacturing industries underlined the colony's dependence for revenue on the importation of goods for the Transvaal market. Despite the rupturing of that trade during the second Anglo-Boer War, the presence of imperial troops in the colony had brought unprecedented prosperity to Natal. The ministry of Sir Albert Hime had used the opportunity offered by the war and by a subsequent boom to embark on ambitious schemes of railway and harbour construction. Government expenditure soared and the cost of administration increased both to cover current expenses and to finance loans.

In 1903, the boom collapsed and the colony, in common with the rest of the subcontinent, was caught up in an acute economic depression. Not only was Natal saddled with considerable debts, she was also confronted with a situation where the new British administration in the Transvaal was favouring the Portuguese port of Lourenço Marques over that of Durban. This resulted in a considerable loss of both customs and railway revenue which exacerbated the financial crisis in the colony. In 1907, the year before Lamb wrote *Hard Times*, the depression was deepened by the start of a world-wide recession.

The crisis gripping the colony was further complicated by a succession of natural disasters which had wreaked havoc on agricultural production since the early 1890s. Intermittent droughts and locust plagues had destroyed crops while, in the late 1890s, colonial herds had been devastated by rinderpest. In 1904, a tick-borne disease, east coast fever, had broken out in northern Natal. By 1908, it was widespread in both white- and African-owned herds. The dairy industry, which had promised to become an important source of revenue, was particularly hard hit by east coast fever.

In 1908, confronted with this situation, R.H. Lamb placed his observations and remedies before the Natal public. *Hard Times in Natal and the Way Out* offers an interesting if provocative and, at times, distinctly unconventional analysis. Some of Lamb's comments provide useful and penetrating observations of the state of affairs in late-colonial Natal, yet his advice is not always practical and indeed it frequently verges on the eccentric. Suggestions such as the opening up of the rural districts by a network of electric trams and the overcoming of the social isolation of the farmers by means of a system of telephones[3] beg the question whether Lamb was always as serious as he appears to be or whether his advice was sometimes rather tongue in cheek.

But in general, Lamb offers a number of unexceptional remedies. No one can quibble with his assertion that more scientific farming methods were needed to enable Natal to feed her population, or with his demand for a thorough and free educational system for the colony. But these were long-term remedies and indeed he makes no suggestion as to how they could be achieved or financed. Some of his proposals for immediate reform are equally unexceptional yet again, given the circumstances of the time, not always practicable.

In keeping with contemporary wisdom, he urges the adoption of a high protective tariff to enable Natal to protect her own interests and establish and maintain industries. While the movement towards protectionism was already firmly established in most of the industrializing countries, free trade still remained the dominant ideology of the ruling Liberal Party in London. For Natal to adopt protectionist tariffs, which would have discriminated against British goods, would have aroused considerable opposition. A more immediate counter to a protectionist policy was the fact that since 1903, Natal had been united in a customs union with the other British colonies in southern Africa. Practically, therefore, Lamb's 'way out' could not be implemented.

Lamb's comments on the inequalities inherent in the colonial system of taxation are more apposite. The only direct taxes in the colony fell on the black races and particularly on the Africans whose main contribution to revenue was in the form of an annual hut tax. By 1905, faced with a soaring deficit, the Natal administration under the premiership of Charles Smythe had desperately tried to increase revenue. It had few options other than a direct tax on the settler community, yet attempts to introduce a property tax and income tax were thrown out by Parliament. In 1905, aware that no tax which did not also increase the amount paid by the black races would be accepted by the settlers, the government introduced a poll tax to be payable by all adult males in the colony other than those homestead heads who paid hut taxes.

The main burden of the poll tax fell on the Africans and the widespread hostility which they felt towards it had sparked off the Bhambatha Rebellion of 1906. More even than the hut tax, it symbolized the injustice of a system whereby whites with an average per capita income over 30 times greater than that of Africans, paid no direct taxes. By contrast, the average African labourer paid a high proportion of his annual wages in direct taxes.[4] Lamb is well aware of the injustice inherent in this situation and he demands the introduction of a more equitable system of taxation, singling out the poll tax for special censure.

The absence of a properly designed property tax was possibly the most important contributory fact to the stagnation of the colonial economy. It encouraged the inefficient use of farm land and militated against agricultural development. Lamb realizes this and advocates the introduction of a tax on properties of over 100 acres. Yet he fails to take into account the realities of a situation in which all effective power within the colony was exercised by that section of the population on which a property tax would fall most directly; the white farmers.

Until 1893, Natal had been governed by officials appointed by the Colonial Office in London. In that year the colony had been granted responsible government under a constitution which placed effective power in the hands of a parliament in which representation was heavily loaded in favour of the settler farming interest. If Lamb hoped to influence official opinion, he had to take into account the influence wielded by the farming interest.

Even a cursory glance at the pamphlet shows that this could not have been his intention. He delights in his attacks on the farmers' representatives, dismissing them as 'rustics from the rural regions who are out of touch with the world's doings and who really know no more about the science of government than they know about the science of navigation'. They are 'the most unbusinesslike, slipshod, haphazard set of people . . . fifty years behind the age in agricultural matters and a hundred years behind in governmental affairs'.[5]

Despite the flamboyance of his language and despite his condemnation of parliamentarians as demagogues and of the government as an oligarchy, there was much justice in Lamb's strictures on Natal's politicians and particularly on his judgement that radical changes could be brought about only if there were a change in the type of men elected to Parliament. Far too many Members of Parliament were opportunistic and self-seeking, concerned more with protecting their own sectional interests than with providing good government for the colony. Between 1898 and 1910, political life was characterized by a series of unstable coalitions in which district rivalries played a greater role than did political persuasions. Despite the election of four Labour members in 1906, there were no clearly defined political parties and the frequent change of ministries did not herald the adoption of new policies. According to the Governor, Sir Matthew Nathan, the settlers governed 'themselves badly . . . and the native population worse'.[6]

The treatment by the ministries and Parliament of the African race was, indeed, the greatest accusation which could be held against the settlers. And it is one which Lamb employs to the full. His indictment of official policy towards both the Africans and the Indians reveals the extent of the gulf between the Yankee newcomer to Natal and the white society in which he found himself. Few colonists expressed his sense of outrage at the treatment meted out to the black races while even those who did would not have shared his conviction that 'civilized' Africans and Indians should be given equality with white settlers. In a climate of deteriorating race relations and of growing racial stereotypes, Lamb's indictment of official policy is particularly apposite. He places the blame for the deterioration on the shoulders of the Members of Parliament who, if 'they were patriots and statesmen . . . would not descend to the ignoble principle of stirring up strife and discord, creating racial hatred . . .'[7]

In general, the growing racial prejudice within white society tended to be directed against the Indians. Using the powers given to them by responsible government, successive ministries had passed a series of laws and measures designed to defuse the economic and political threats which they perceived to be posed by the Indians. Amongst the measures was the repatriation to India of ex-indentured labourers. Lamb firmly rejects this and argues that the Indian has both a moral and a legal right to stay in Natal. Lamb opposes all attempts to classify people according to racial stereotypes and argues instead that their ability as labourers should be the criterion. Using this as a yardstick, the Indian is the ideal citizen: 'His tendency is towards industry and thrift . . . [and he] is the personification of industry and economy . . . The Indians instead of being a curse to the country . . . are in reality one of its greatest blessings.'[8] Yet despite this, Lamb realizes that continuing Indian immigration would cause an increase in racial feeling and, to avoid this, he calls for an end to immigration.

The prominent place Lamb accords to the Indian population in his pamphlet and his sympathetic treatment of their plight could be a result of the years he had spent in the East. His empathy with Indians is manifest and it is interesting to note that an Indian firm, P.S. Aiyar of Durban, printed *Hard Times*.[9] Yet, despite the prominence he accords to the Indians, Lamb correctly identifies the 'Native Question' as one of the great issues facing Natal. By 1908, the treatment meted out to the African population had done much to undermine stability in the colony and to prevent progress. Shula Marks has described the settlers' attitude to the Africans as a 'curious blend of paternalism, fear and contempt'.[10] All avenues to progress and prosperity had been relentlessly closed and the stranglehold both of officialdom and of the farming community tightened. The mid-Victorian emergence of a Christianized, petty bourgeois African class, the *Kholwa*, to take its place alongside the settler community had been reversed and its members were in the process of being pushed back into the wider African community. Through a tightly regulated 'tribal' system, the settlers exercised a wide-ranging control over most aspects of African life.

It was a control buttressed by laws and regulations which had turned a considerable part of the African population into a class of lawbreakers and criminals. Lamb was not the first white to criticize the viciousness and counter-productiveness of such a form of control and his condemnation echoes that of Joseph Baynes's published attack on government policy in 1906.[11] Lamb shares Baynes's conviction that Africans had been driven to rebellion in 1906 through a combination of prejudice, racial hatred and misgovernment but in his remedy for African grievances he goes much further. Like other white philanthropists in the colony, Baynes was essentially a segregationist, believing that Africans were incapable of assimilation into settler society. To Lamb, the question of African control is far more simply resolved into one of two propositions 'They must either be civilised or exterminated'.[12] He argues that both from the economic and the practical point of view, 'civilizing' the African is the cheapest and best thing to do. In order to achieve this, Lamb calls for compulsory education for all Africans between six and fifteen years and draws a clear correlation between civilization and the work ethic.

Hand in hand with education, Lamb stresses the need for treating Africans with absolute justice. Here, too, he goes further than the philanthropists were prepared to go. While advocating the more usual remedies such as protecting Africans from the incompetence and bias of white judges and juries, and from the tentacles of money-lenders, he equates justice with doing everything possible to place Africans on an equal footing with the settlers. Lamb the American demands acceptance of the fundamental principle that all 'just powers of government are derived from the consent of the governed'.[13] He sees education as the only sensible criterion of the right of franchise and looks forward to the day when all suitably educated people in Natal, black and white, male and female, should have the vote.

This is Lamb at his idealistic best, demanding acceptance of a system of justice which he knows will be rejected out of hand by the colony's ruling class. Yet Lamb the pragmatist is once again clearly evident. Just as he advocated ending Indian immigration but insisted on treating those in the colony justly, so he offers to his readers his conviction that equality of African and white would ultimately reduce the threat of competition. Despite all the evidence to the contrary, he accepts the arguments of Southern academics in the United States that the African Americans were dying out from inherent and natural causes, and believes the same to be true for the Africans: 'The Natives would not materially increase, they would tend more to diminish under domestic improvement. They would be civilised to extinction.'[14]

It is needless to say that Lamb's remedies for Natal's problems were never put to the test. Few of them were economically or practically possible while hardly any would have received a sympathetic hearing from the colony's white population. Settler interest in his pamphlet appears to have been slight. There was no public official response while the *Natal Mercury* dismissed it with scorn, playing on those features of the pamphlet which were patently absurd. Significantly, as a newspaper in the vanguard of anti-Indian agitation in the colony, the *Mercury* concentrated its attack on those aspects which dealt with the Indian position and the reviewer singled out as significant the fact that it was printed by an Indian firm.[15]

Ironically, *Hard Times in Natal and the Way Out* appeared shortly before the onset of an economic upswing in 1909, close on the heels of a similar recovery in Britain. Lamb had strongly advocated a coming together of the South African colonies as the surest remedy for Natal's problems and would have approved the steady progress after 1908 which culminated in the proclamation of the Union of South Africa on 31 May 1910. Whether he was still in Natal to celebrate the event is uncertain. In February 1908 he had appealed to the Supreme Court to have his name restored to the Dental Register. His appeal had been dismissed[16] and it is possible that he had then moved on to pastures new. The establishment of the Union did prove a 'way out' to Natal's 'hard times' yet Lamb would surely not have approved of the fact that it provided essentially a 'way out' for the settler community and served to cement the subordinate position of Africans and Indians within a racially-based and white-dominated oligarchy.

John Lambert

NOTES

1. *The Natal who's who: an illustrated biographical sketch of Natalians* (Durban, 1906), p.113; *Natal Witness*, 26 February 1908.
2. A. Duminy and B. Guest, 'The Anglo-Boer war and its economic aftermath, 1899–1910', in A. Duminy and B. Guest, (eds), *Natal and Zululand, from earliest times to 1910: a new history* (Pietermaritzburg, 1989), p.358.
3. *Hard times*, pp.12–13, 29.
4. Duminy and Guest, p.367.
5. *Hard times*, p.4.
6. Quoted in S. Marks, *Reluctant rebellion: the 1906–1908 disturbances in Natal* (Oxford, 1970), p.19.
7. *Hard times*, p.23.
8. *Hard times*, pp.19, 23.
9. *Natal Mercury*, 12 March 1908.
10. Marks, p.11.

11. J. Baynes, *Letters addressed to His Excellency the Governor of Natal, and His Majesty's Secretary of State for the Colonies, regarding the absence of consideration in our present form of government for our coloured population* (Reprint, Pietermaritzburg, 1992).
12. *Hard times*, p. 14.
13. *Hard times*, p. 24.
14. *Hard times*, p. 28.
15. *Natal Mercury*, 12 March 1908.
16. *Natal Witness*, 27 February 1908.

HARD TIMES

IN

NATAL

AND

THE WAY OUT

By

Dr. R. H. LAMB.

PRICE ONE SHILLING.

" Pledge to no Party's Arbitrary Sway.
Follow Truth Wherever it Leads the Way."

R. H. LAMB, D. D. S.

Hard Times in Natal

AND

The Way Out.

Natal, the Garden Colony of South Africa, is one of the fairest portions of the earth. It has a productive soil, a favourable position in the south temperate zone; a sufficient amount of rainfall to produce good crops; a wide range of altitude from sea level to six thousand feet elevation which renders it capable of great diversity of products, and one of the finest climates to be met with in any part of the world.

There are many reasons why it should be an eminently prosperous country, and one of the most desirable to live in. Its resources are great and comparatively undeveloped. It is sparsely populated and, therefore, affords wonderful opportunities for the few who inhabit it. It has a sound money system, and no need of expensive administration of government. It has no army or navy to support, no pensions to pay, not even poor houses to maintain. It has cheap labour, and plenty of work for all.

There are also some reasons why it is not more prosperous than it is at present.

Like everything else it is subject to the law of cause and effect. There are underlying causes sufficient to produce the present state of financial and commercial depression, one of which is the necessary reaction incident to the artificial condition created by a tremendous war and inflated values induced by a sudden influx of capital and population, which from the nature of things must of necessity react and create a lull equal to the exhilaration and over stimulation of war times. That the condition of affairs is not very much worse is a matter of good fortune that deserves great satisfaction, for it is entirely too much to expect that this country should be an exception to all others in its experience with warfare. We have the examples of Russia and Japan before us. They are just now suffering from the aftermath incident to a conflict at arms. The United States of America is another example. After the war of the rebellion it was for a time almost paralysed in its financial and industrial life. It took years to recuperate its lost vitality, and it will also take this country a while to regain its normal condition.

It has an uncivilised race to deal with as a menace to its health, development and safety. It has droughts and pests to contend with and some other drawbacks, but its greatest obstacle is the inefficient administration of governmental affairs. No country on earth could prosper with

A Hayseed Government

such as we have in this beautiful land. A government made up of rustics from the rural regions who are out of touch with the world's doings and who really know no more about the science of government than they know about the science of navigation. They are in reality no more capable of playing the part of a statesman and a legislator than they are of enacting the role of a doctor, a lawyer, or a school teacher. It is a notable fact that farmers are the most unbusinesslike, slipshod, haphazard set of people that can be found in any country. Everything they do is by rule of thumb method that would be ruinous to any other class of business men. The farmers of this country are fifty years behind the age in agricultural matters and a hundred years behind in governmental affairs, and yet they essay to carry on a parliament and enact laws that they suppose will successfully conduct the country through the vicissitudes of misfortune and restore it to a condition of ordinary prosperity. Their inability to do this is being demonstrated day by day, and while they are attempting it the country is suffering for want of wise and able measures of actual statesmanship.

Without some radical change is made, disastrous results will ultimately ensue. State affairs will continue to be in a muddle so long as the muddlers are depended upon to extricate it from the deplorable condition that it is now in, and the probability is that things will go right on getting worse rather than better for want of competent heads and hands at the helm. There are good and able men to be found here who are capable of successfully conducting business either in their own interests or in the interests of the country. They, no doubt, have a comprehensive idea as to what ought to be done and how to do it, but they are not in politics. They do not put themselves forward, harangue a crowd, and blow and bluster as the typical politician is wont to do, but they think, and make mental criticism of the political wind bags and puff stuff orators who have some personal axe to grind and in reality are not actuated by patriotic motives. They care nothing for the country so long as their personal ambition and purposes are served.

There are doubtless men of independent means who have no need to make a living out of politics, and would not prostitute their trust to any mercenary or selfish ends were they to be placed in so responsible a position, and who could be induced to assume such civic duties if they were sought for and assured of the confidence of the people. The ordinary method of allowing candidates to electioneer for office is radically wrong and should be abolished and reversed. In order to get the best men into official life it is the right thing that

The Office Should Seek The Man.

The very fact of a candidate for office trying to get the people to take him up and support him is quite sufficient reason why he should be turned down with vehemence.

What would be thought of the medical doctor who would go about blowing his horn and trying to get people to take his medicine? He would be regarded as a quack and given the go by, but the political doctor goes abroad in the land with his panacea and succeeds in foisting himself upon the body politic. More is the pity! Good physicians are always sought for and applied to for advice, and the political physician is equally retiring and equally capable of giving valuable aid when called upon by a confiding public.

This ought to be one of the most prosperous countries in the world, and could very readily be made so if its inhabitants would only go the right way about it.

The First Important Measure

towards the development and ultimate success of the country is the federation of the whole of South Africa into a centralised government with each colony represented in a parliament proportionate to its population. This undoubtedly is the ultimate destiny of the country, but its consummation may be long delayed, and until that desirable end shall have been reached each colony must do all that it can towards individual development and progress, but that it will be able to reach a very important position among the countries of the world is not at all probable. Centralisation of government is the modern method of conducting matters of state. The German Empire never amounted to anything so long as its component parts remained separate provinces and principalities of no special importance.

The Japanese Empire also amounted to nothing under the old feudal system during the reign of the Dameos. Australia is another example. It could make no material progress so long as its separate states were competing one against another, in the way of maintaining free trade in one section and a protective tariff in another.

Now that it is united and agreed upon a principle of national policy it will progress as it never could have otherwise done. Under a united government South Africa is capable of producing wonderful possibilities, and that should be the aim and aspiration of its respective states. By confederation and good management a commonwealth could be built up that would take rank among the foremost countries of the world. The measure to be the most beneficial to this and all the other South African Colonies would be a policy of instituting and maintaining a system of

High Protective Tariff.

It is to be admitted, of course, that the free trade principle is the correct one and should be adopted the world over. Every port in every country should be wide open to the free commerce of the world, but since that very much to be desired state of affairs is at present unattainable, and the great majority of all other countries are acting upon the protective principle and are likely to continue to do so for a long while yet, it is expedient that this country should in its own interests play at the same game and thereby put itself upon a self sustaining basis. In no other way can home industries be established and successfully maintained. The whole trouble of the present financial straits has been brought about by the fact that we import too much and export too little. The country lives beyond its means. Take the daily routine of the average business man of Durban and it will illustrate the point. From the time he arises in the morning from his bed, made in Birmingham, until he retires to the same in the evening he is a patron of foreign industries. Every article of his toilette, except the water, is a foreign product; his breakfast is probably made up of Quaker Oats from America, bread made of Australian flour and spread with New Zealand butter, his mutton chop is the cold storage imported article, his tea is from Ceylon and is sweetened by Mauritius sugar and condensed milk from Switzerland, his bacon comes from the western prairies of America, and though he is amidst the abundant fruits of the garden colony his marmalade and his jam come from abroad; every article of his festive board from the table to the tea spoons are of foreign manufacture; the paper he reads and the ink it is printed with comes from Europe; every article of clothing he wears is from the same locality;

the tram car he rides in is imported; the desk he sits down to is American; the piano he listens to is European; and pretty much everything that he consumes and depends upon is imported except air and water. He believes in patronising everybody in every other country except Natal, which he expects under these conditions ought to afford him a good living, and is disappointed when he does not get it. The present system of low custom duties is a detriment to the country, for the reason that is has no protective tendency either to create or maintain home industries, and simply amounts to a tax and permits a tremendous amount of money to be spent out of the country that ought to be retained. It does not admit of any attempt to produce here in competition with old established industries in densely populated countries that consume practically an unlimited output. In sparsely populated countries like this a larger profit is necessary on a proportionately small output. Nothing, therefore, but a high duty is going to protect the small manufacturer and enable him to compete with the small profit on large output principle in vogue in other countries. No infant industry would survive its second summer in competing with the gigantic industries of other countries which practically have a free market here. The difference of a small percentage does not affect them because it is paid by the consumer.

This country could and should have its own industries. Its natural products provide the raw materials for many important manufactures. It seems ridiculous to produce wool here, send it seven thousand miles to market, where it is made up into clothing, blankets, etc., and then bring it back another seven thousand miles and pay twelve or fifteen per cent. duty on it after it has been by foreign labour enhanced ten times in value, and then consumed right here where it ought to have remained and been manufactured into clothing. And again, hides are produced here, exported and again imported at a high figure in the form of leather goods. Even the bark for tanning it abroad is produced here and exported along with the hide.

Why Not Have Tanneries Here!

and cloth, and shoe manufactories also? It is prevented only by low custom duties on manufactured articles that could and would undersell the local manufacturer. Yet this is not conducive to the development, progress, and prosperity of this country. It would be far better if all such imported articles were barred out of the local market by a tariff sufficiently high to give the Natal man a chance, even though shoes and such things should be enhanced somewhat in price thereby. Everybody would be indirectly benefitted because the money would stay here and circulate throughout the country instead of going into the coffers of the foreign manufacturer, and thus creating a monetary condition here like unto Mother Hubbard's Cupboard.

A great many people have the idea that anything that is produced at home is necessarily inferior to something of the same kind that comes from a far away country; the further it comes and the more it costs the better it must be, and they are willing to pay a third more than a thing is really worth because it is the product of a foreign country. People who can afford luxuries are obviously the ones to pay for them. Those who think that they must of necessity array themselves in silks, satins and fine raiment, should not grumble at the cost thereof even if a good percentage of it goes towards the upkeep of the government. The necessities and the ordinary comforts of life should be made as cheap as possible. It is all very well for people to ride in motor cars if they can afford to do so, but if the import duty on such things was sufficient to enhance their cost considerably beyond the home made product it is very natural to suppose that many people would content themselves with domestic industry that would otherwise import their cars, and export the money to pay for them. On the same principle let those who indulge in the luxury of music pay well for their imported pianos or else play on Jew's harps until such time as a piano factory is started that can turn out a good home product at moderate cost.

Natal ought to be in reality a flourishing manufacturing country; it has the natural advantages to warrant it. It is the producer of many kinds of raw material that could be utilised for manufacturing purposes; it has numerous streams and cataracts that could be used to generate electrical motor power sufficient to run all the countless wheels of industrial toil that could be set in motion; there is cheap and efficient Indian labour that could be employed and rendered very valuable. Cloth, clothing, boots and shoes, furniture, soap, candles, carriages, harness, matches, medicines and many other things of daily use could be manufactured right here in sufficient quantities to meet the local demand and even for export in some instances. There should be a high import duty on anything of that kind that can be produced here, but raw materials and such things as cannot very well be produced should be duty free.

As an Agricultural Country

this ought to be one of the best in the world. The climate is unexcelled in any part of the earth, and the soil will yield abundantly if properly tilled.

Such a thing as scientific farming is entirely unknown here, and will continue to be an unknown art so long as no pains are taken to inculcate the necessary knowledge. There are wonderful possibilities open for enterprise in many agricultural ways that have not yet been entered into. It is as a fact one of the first fruit countries of the world and could very easily become a rival of California, which is now the fruit garden of America. It has natural advantages that are possessed by very few countries; it has sufficient rainfall to insure good crops and the altitude, latitude and climatic conditions to suit a very great variety of the finest fruits that grow. There are localities here adapted to almost any kind of fruit that is desired. At Bulwer, 5,000 feet altitude, California plums grow to perfection and frequently attain to the extraordinary size of six inches in circumference. Apples, pears, quinces, and many other fruits incident to the temperate zone also flourish surprisingly well. These fruits if grown in large quantities would find ready sale in European markets in their fresh state and could also be evaporated by modern methods and exported profitably. There are millions of beautiful fertile acres over which a few straggling herds wander which are capable of producing sufficient to maintain ten times the present population of the country, held by a few land barons who like the dog in the manger will neither use it themselves nor allow any one else to do so, and the hapless residents are necessitated to purchase at high prices from the producer over the seas the very things which could and ought to be produced right here in abundance and sold at half the price.

It seems perfectly ridiculous for a country like this, with its green pastures and fertile valleys, to import its butter, cheese, mutton and beef.

The Farmer

is too little protected in some ways and too much in others. If there was a shilling a pound duty on butter and cheese it would create a home market for such farm produce at about the price of the imported article, and the money paid for it would stay in the country and be in circulation. It is urged that the home product is deficient in quality; this need not necessarily be the case if there is an incentive for improvement created by a protective tariff. The milk is of good quality and there is, therefore, no good reason why the butter should not be also when there is a demand for it. There is always a good demand for a good quality at a good price, and those who produced the inferior article would have to accept an inferior price for it until they learned the art of good butter making. The people who have such aesthetic tastes that they cannot subsist on the products of the country and think they require their food brought from abroad, are the ones to pay for their gratification and delusion in the way of taxes on imports. The farmer is justly entitled to his share of protection, and he should also be expected to contribute his share in bearing the expenses necessary to carry on the government. There is no good reason why he should be allowed to hold a tremendous amount of land unoccupied and unused free of tax. So long as he pays nothing he has no incentive to cultivate and earn and be able to contribute to the expenses of state. If direct taxation is necessary it is obvious that somebody must pay taxes. A government cannot be run without money any more than a boat can be run without water. The question, therefore, arises what are

The Best Means of Raising Revenue?

There are two methods of taxation, direct and indirect; of the former there is poll tax, and tax on property and on income; of the latter there is stamp duties, licences and custom duties. The most of these methods constitute a very inequitable system of taxation. The poll tax particularly is very unequal since the kafir who earns only a pound a month pays just as much tax as the M.L.A. who gets a pound a day, but in reality earns nothing. An income tax has its objections also because it creates an incentive to fraud and evasions; it necessitates an odious kind of espionage and inquisitiveness into people's private affairs. As Gladstone[1] has said, it tends to make a nation of liars. The honest, straightforward people have to not only pay their own share of taxes but also pay for those who wriggle out of paying. It also necessitates an elaborate system of private book keeping in order to know just what amount of income people have. The dishonest sharper could and would juggle with figures in such a way that they would not know how much income tax should be paid. By such a system those who could in reality pay the most would actually pay the least, and those who could ill afford taxation would be the ones who would have to bear the burden.

The licence system is also a very unequal kind of taxation as it bears the heaviest upon those who are the least able to stand it; it is discouraging to the beginner in a small way to be subject to the same amount of taxation as the old established and prosperous merchant or professional man; it is out of all sense of proportion to require a man conducting a small retail establishment confined to one line of goods only, to pay an equal amount of licence as the mammoth department store comprising a dozen or more lines of goods, all on a large scale, and representing on the whole a volume of business twenty or thirty times greater than the one line store on a small scale. For this country and the whole of South Africa the indirect system of taxation by means of import duties is the most desirable and should be adopted so long as the present conditions exist and the other countries of the world are not yet ready to adopt a system of universal free trade, which ought to be brought about as soon as possible for it is without doubt the correct thing. High duties should exist on anything and everything that can be produced here, but no duty at all on things which tend to the improvement and development of the country such as art, education, clocks, watches, stoves, dishes, medicines, surgical appliances, optical goods, books, stationery, plants, seeds, stock or poultry for breeding purposes, etc., etc. The aim should be to have the necessities of life as cheap as possible and let the luxuries and superfluities be the expensive things and contribute to the revenue of the country.

If this policy were pursued enough money could be obtained from imports alone to carry on the expenses of the government and at the same time all kinds of home industries would spring up all over the country. Labour would be in demand; everybody would be employed and instead of people leaving the country they would all stay and others would come. Natal would be the Eldorado of the southern seas. If more money than that derived from custom duties should be required however, the best method of direct taxation would be a property tax. Let property of all kinds whether it consists of houses or lands, or hotels or cattle, or mines or bonds, be subject to taxation in proportion to its value; that is a tax which cannot possibly be evaded, and is derived from those able to pay. It is simply a matter of assessment and collection and requires no complicated system of finding out who ought to pay and who not; simply an assessor and a collector of each county is sufficient. All unoccupied and uncultivated land should be assessed at its productive value. Since land is so plentiful and cheap and population so small comparatively, it would be admissable to exempt a hundred acres from taxation so that people could build up small homesteads and maintain them free of tax, but all over a hundred acres owned by any one individual should be taxed at a perfectly safe valuation whether it is cultivated or not; if it is not, taxation would naturally cause it to be. Large landed proprietors, who have bitten off more than they can chew, would then have to hustle or sell out. In order to guard against grumblers the government should make a standing offer to take over land at double its assessed value at any time and pay out cash for it, which it should improve by irrigation and other ways, and then sell to people of small means who want to build homes for themselves and their families on easy terms or long lease.

These two systems of taxation would produce all the revenue required because the government need not be run on expensive lines. There are many ways of retrenchment that could very profitably be adopted; the Legislative Assembly could be reduced in numbers by one half and be improved thereby, its present large number of bunglers is an illustration of too many cooks spoiling the broth; half the number at half the pay would do more effectual and profitable work. The position should be more honorary than remunerative. It is properly a place for men of independent means who have no personal ends to further and who accept the position from patriotic rather than mercenary motives.

The Licence System Should Be Abolished

because it is unnecessary, unjust, and an unfair discrimination against the professional class and tends to discourage rather than promote higher education. A young lawyer who may have exhausted his financial resources in the pursuit of his studies, before he is able to begin practice and put himself in the way of earning a penny, is requested to pay the government about seventy pounds for the privilege of making an honourable living. There is no justice in requiring a young struggling professional man, trying to make an honourable living in the way that he is best adapted by means of his education, to pay cash down in advance a considerable sum called licence by courtesy but in reality a direct tax to the government, while the land baron has his thousands of arable acres surrounding his sumptuous homestead, and his flocks and herds and carriages and horses, is not asked to contribute a single penny beyond the poll tax, which the professional man also pays to defray the governmental expenses. Such is the odious class legislation of this country. One of the greatest obstacles to the development of this country is

Poor Transportation Facilities

and the fact of railways being a government monopoly is responsible for it. No country is so well served by government management as by private enterprise. The freight rates are so high that many farm products go to waste rather than to market. Cheap transportation is very much needed and could be had by allowing private companies to construct their own roads through such sections of country as need them. A cheap system of roads could be constructed and conducted on the electric tram system that would work wonders in the opening up of remote rural districts that need only means of transit to render them desirable as places of residence and profitable for farming purposes. They should traverse the length and breadth of the country. Their construction and maintenance is so comparatively small that every locality could be supplied. Little grading is required as they can run up hill and down dale; no expensive stations to construct; no great staff of employees to maintain. Double deck cars could be run, with the lower part arranged for the carriage of freight and the upper for passengers; the latter could be carried at halfpenny a mile at a good profit and freight in proportion. The numerous cataracts all over the country are provided by nature as power stations to generate all the electricity that would be needed. With roads of this description farm lands would be wonderfully enhanced in value and fruits and such perishable products as now never see the markets, because to send them there costs more than they come to, could all be profitably sold and everything could be utilised. The existing steam roads could be still used for through freight and passengers to remote parts but all the local transportation could be effectually and cheaply carried on by electric trams. Then small farms would pay, and people would be glad to live on them.

Another Great Need

of the country is a thorough free educational system that would ensure a good common school education to every child throughout the land. It is an institution that no country at this day and age can afford to do without. It has been the making of Germany; it has made America great; it is reconstructing and regenerating Japan; and it will do wonders for Natal if the people will have the gumption to adopt it. No expenditure of public money will pay anything to compare with that which is devoted to the education of the populace. There is no way in which the government can so well afford to be lavish with its wealth as building and maintaining school houses. It can afford to neglect the building of highways and bridges, the construction of costly buildings, but it cannot afford to neglect the intellectual development of its youth. If there is any one thing that this country stands in need of more than another it is general education; for it is the foundation of all civilisation and human progress. There should not only be free common schools started all over the country, but a number of technical schools where young men and women could learn useful trades, and also an agricultural college, where scientific farming could be learned.

That is the only way to keep abreast of the times, and if such important matters are neglected the country is sure to suffer in consequence. Nothing but an autocratic government can ever be successfully maintained in a country containing an illiterate populace. Democracy is the product of intelligence, and is the only true foundation of liberty. Illiteracy is a menace to public safety. An educational qualification is the only sensible criterion of the right of franchise, and this admits of the advisability of

Woman Suffrage,

which every civilised country must of necessity and will eventually adopt. Natal has a grand opportunity to distinguish itself and improve itself, by joining the vanguard of human progress by its recognition of this inevitable fact. It would give it a boot forward and a prestige that would be far reaching in its effects, but as there is so little probability of its being brought about very soon, it is scarcely worth the while to discuss at length the many very manifest advantages that would accrue. The justice of the recognition of woman's influence and material aid in all matters of State could be dilated upon very profitably if the male populace of the country only had an ear to hear. Unfortunately it is, however, deaf and dumb and blind to its own interests in that direction, and will have to grope its way through political darkness for years yet to come before it is ready to admit the light of truth that will illuminate its path. Though this subject may be kept in abeyance and its importance unrecognised and ignored, it is destined to ultimately come to the front and claim the consideration that it so justly deserves. There are, however, other important matters and problems confronting the country which cannot be overlooked, conspicuous among which is

THE NATIVE QUESTION,

which is of great and grave magnitude, and requires thoughtful consideration. It does not admit of any errors of omission or of commission without their entailing consequences of serious import.

Whatever may be said or done regarding the native population of the country, the whole question is resolved into one of two propositions. They must either be civilised or exterminated. Their ways are not our ways, and so long as things remain as they are there will be wars and rumours of wars. In their present state of semi-barbarism they cannot be brought to an understanding of the mysterious modes and methods of the white man. They represent the intellectual childhood of the human race, and it is unreasonable to expect that they can suddenly reach the same stage of development that the European has attained through centuries of intellectual growth. They constitute a very large proportion of the population and the masses of them are in dense ignorance, and dominated by gross superstition. Ignorance in any form always constitutes a serious menace to the State. It is not amenable to reason, nor can it be controlled by lawful measures. If they were governed by the unerring hand of justice it would help matters amazingly. But, unfortunately, they are not, and they are not too obtuse to recognise that fact. The recent report of the Commissioners bear out this statement. Even a child is quick to discern injustice. They have no representation whatever and yet are taxed very much more heavily than the white man in proportion to their respective wealth.

Extracted from the Native Commission Report.

REVENUE FROM NATIVES, 1906.[2]

Hut Tax	...	...	...	...	£121,374	18	7
Dog „	...	...	...	...	15,507	10	0
Poll „	...	...	...	...	68,500	1	0
Squatters Rent		...	...	...	4,499	19	0
Pass Fees	...	...	...	...	3,694	12	0
Medical Licence Fees	...	...	...	2,539	0	0
Marriage „ „	...	...	...	454	10	0
Fines and Court Fees	...	...	...	28,695	4	7
Total ...	...	...	...	£245,695	14	7

They are not consulted in the making or administration of the laws; they are frequently punished for the violation of laws they are in total ignorance of; they are often the victims of prejudice and racial hatred on the part of some colonial magistrates, and fined and flogged unreasonably for slight provocation. Their punishment is not infrequently out of all proportion to the gravity of the offence, and would not be meted out to a white man under the same circumstances. When such things exist it is not to be wondered at that discontent and a spirit of rebellion should be created. To resent wrong and injustice is human nature, no matter how high a state of civilisation may have been reached. Both the white and the black man are here, and they are here to stay. The latter constitutes the white man's burden, and he should endeavour to arise to the responsibility that Nature has placed upon him. At this day and age waging a war of extermination is utterly out of the question and need not be considered. The only alternative left, therefore, is to civilise the native and thus insure permanent peace and prosperity. It is the cheapest and best thing to do from an economic standpoint. The late rebellion cost the country £750,000 and ignorance is responsible for the whole thing. No civilised natives were implicated in the affair, presumably for the reason that they are sufficiently enlightened to understand the utter futility of attempting to cope with the white man.

A raw kafir has no conception of things as they are. He believes what the witch doctors tell him regarding immunity from bullets, and he never finds out his mistake until he is dead. Intelligence is the only antidote for the poison of superstition. It is desirable and advisable to sufficiently civilise the natives that they may become peaceable and industrious members of the body politic, and the way to civilise them is to educate them. If this £750,000 had been spent on education ten years ago, it would have founded and maintained 750 schools during the last decade, and in consequence no rebellion could have come off. School houses and teachers and books are a better investment than machine guns and explosive bullets. They are both effective in their way, but the former represent the better way.

The natives are justly entitled to the advantage of primary education. They pay taxes and there is no way in which that money could be expended more profitably than by the erection and maintenance of school houses throughout the land. Compulsory attendance of every child between six and fifteen years should be the law. The State owes this as a duty to every child born within its precincts, and when it has discharged that duty, it can with some degree of grace require an observance of law, order and industry.

A rudimentary education would result in the creation of wants incident to civilised life, and it would suggest industrious and abstemious habits as the means by which those wants are acquired. With an appreciation of the value of labour as a means of satisfying the requirements of civilised life, the native would become a most valuable asset to this country, and contribute wonderfully to its development and its material progress.

Apropos to this important subject of education I append some statistical facts taken from "The American Year Book" to show what is being done in the former slave states of the South towards the amelioration of the negro race there, with some comments as to the value of an educational system for the common people printed in connection therewith.

"In 1902 the common school enrolment in colored schools in the sixteen former slave states and the district of Columbia numbered 1,587,309. In 1877, the first year in which the statistics of the colored schools were taken separately, there were 571,506 colored pupils and 1,827,139 white pupils in the schools of the South. This number increased to 2,215,678 white pupils and 784,709 colored pupils in 1880. In 1890 the white pupils of the sixteen former slave states had increased to 3,402,420, and the colored pupils had increased to 1,296,959. The increase, therefore, in the past thirteen years of white pupils has been nearly 1,300,000 and colored pupils 440,000. The expenditure from taxation for the public schools of both races in these sixteen states amounted to $37,567,552 in the year 1902. The total amount of public taxes expended during the period beginning in 1876 and ending in 1902 for white and colored has been $687,691,329, of which it is estimated that more than $125,000,000 has been expended to support the common schools for negro children.

The illiterate person knows language or speech only by the ear. As all people do their thinking mostly in words, the illiterate person may be said to be ear-minded. When a person comes to know language by the ear he gains in ability in learning the experience of other fellow-beings—such an experience as the highest brute animal is debarred from. For by the use of speech each person may live vicariously over again the lives of other people. He may, by hearing them tell their experiences, their observations, reflections and deeds, get the net results of their living so that man, even if illiterate, may be properly described as an animal who possesses the power of living several lives in one. Through letters the person becomes eye-minded, and when a person can read without effort he finds himself in possession of a much more accurate mind than is possible in the case of the illiterate. Ear-mindedness, having to keep up, as it does, with the spoken word, and having to depend on the memory of what is spoken, cannot critically examine the statements and descriptions, the definitions and deductions, as it can do when it has before it the printed page. In fact, accurate thinking for the most part becomes possible through eye-mindedness and not through ear-mindedness.

The unskilled labourer does not get good wages in any part of the country. The skilled labourer in the city, using tools and directing machinery, earns and receives an average of double the wages that the farm hand gets.

But machinery is going out from the city to the farm, and the farm, too, needs fewer labourers and can furnish more productions. The surplus farmers set free by this process must go into mechanical industries or into transportation and commerce. Fewer and fewer people are needed for the production of the raw materials of food, clothing and shelter all the world over, thanks to mechanical inventions which are pushing the mere illiterate drudge out of his vocation. He must climb up or else starve in his attempt to compete with the machine.

Here is the wisdom that founds a school system. It makes possible a change of vocations among its people. It puts alertness and versatility in place of mere brute strength and persistency. More than this, the school puts aspiration and ambition into its pupils. The school next proceeds to teach the sciences by which the wonders of the world have been accomplished; mathematics, the tool of thought, by which matter is moved and forces are tamed into the service of man; history, and geography, and grammar, and literature, by which man comes to know men and gains the ability to combine with them in civilised effort.

The city is the necessary resort of the surplus labourers no longer required on the farm. We do not need so many people to get for us the raw materials of food, clothing and shelter, but we need more and more people to turn these raw materials into articles of comfort and luxury; we need more and more people to work at transportation and intercommunication; we need more persons in the work of giving culture to the rest. The savage tribe, unaided by machinery, can afford only one man for the production of ornament; nearly all are needed for the supply of food and clothing of the plainest sort. But the partly civilised tribe can afford ten persons for the production of ornament and luxury. The proportion increases rapidly as we ascend in the use of machinery, and the time is arrived now when more than a hundred in a thousand are needed for the production of ornament and luxury.

In transportation and intercommunication with railroads, telegraphs, postal systems, newspapers, books, libraries, schools and churches—here the line rises from mere transportation through intercommunication up to culture—in these employments more and more workers will be needed.

Here we may see the vast importance of school education in enabling the citizen who shares in the productions of his fellow-men to know his fellows and understand their views of the world. It enables him to know their opinions and to share in their spiritual as well as in their material productions. It enables him to participate in the formation of national and international public opinion.

Small as is the schooling given by our nation to its people—some four and a half years apiece—it suffices to make reading and writing universal, and with them gives also a limited acquaintance with the rudiments of arithmetic and geography. This fits the citizen to become a reader of the daily newspaper and thus brings him under an educating influence that will continue throughout his life. A newspaper civilisation is one that governs by means of public opinion. The newspaper creates public opinion. No great free nation is possible except in a newspaper civilisation."

THE INDIAN QUESTION

is a subject which ought not to constitute any question whatever. The Indian like the European is here, and he has both a moral and a legal right to stay. His tendency is towards industry and thrift. Through centuries of adverse conditions of life he has inherited habits of frugality which enable him to more successfully engage in the struggle for existence than natives of any other country.

We are all the product of pre-natal circumstances and conditions. It is, therefore, just as natural for the Indian coolie to work hard for little pay and to hold on to what he gets no matter how little it may be, and to deprive himself of the comforts of life for the sake of providing against a future emergency, as it is for a kafir to languish in the sunshine wasting his time and energy without thought or care for the morrow. All national and racial characteristics are brought about by a very long train of circumstances extending far back into the dim and distant past.

As in the economy of Nature nothing is ever lost, so it should be in the political economy of a country. Every social element should be so modified and utilised that it would become a factor for the general good. Thus the physical strength of the native would become conducive to the development of the country if by creating new conditions for him, in the way of rudimentary education, he would incline towards industry; and the physique of the coolie in a climate that admits of greater outlay of energy than is possible in the enervating influences of his own country would in the course of time improve to such an extent that he would become an invaluable factor in the industrial life of the colony. The Indian is the personification of industry and economy; he is law abiding and patient in adversity. There is really no reason whatever why he should be made a subject of persecution because he has no vote and cannot, therefore, retaliate upon the agitators and the ranters who rail against him. Therefore public meetings are gotten up, and the notorious demagogues gotten together to harangue the crowds that congregate. They shoot off their mouths with all the force and eloquence at their command in either ignorance or utter disregard of every fundamental principle of national and international law. It is astonishing that men who are old enough and intelligent enough to know better will so deceive themselves that they will publicly give out such absurd and utterly untenable twaddle regarding the Indian population and what should be done to get rid of it. They might with an equal amount of judgment convene a meeting for the purpose of protesting against the Drakensberg mountains and agitating the advisability of their removal from the country.

Anybody unacquainted with existing facts would very naturally infer from their propaganda that this country is a sovereign state, independent and alone capable of framing and enforcing any kinds of laws that it might be inclined to have, and that there is nobody to gainsay them. If this were the case, of course it is to be admitted that all the several schemes and plans that they advocate are quite possible and could be carried out. Fortunately, however, it is otherwise. Natal is simply a fractional and insignificant part of a vast empire; an empire carrying its arts and arms into every continent of the globe and many islands of the sea; an empire made up of many nations, races, creeds, colours, kinds and conditions of men, all built up and cemented together by a constitution which guarantees to all protection of life and property, and equality and impartiality in the administration of the law. It knows of no discrimination in matters of race, religion, or social position.

Such an empire and such a constitution was made possible only by means of maintaining the principles of absolute justice between man and man, and experience has demonstrated the wisdom and the expediency of this. Law, order, and justice is a fixed policy throughout the British dominions that is not likely to be given up or deviated from.

Freedom of thought, speech, and the press is tolerated, and liberty of action is vouchsafed to all; but be it known that the rights and liberties of one leave off where the rights and liberties of another begin. These principles apply to all without distinction of country, creed or colour. If it were not so, it is a question just how long the empire could hold together.

It almost amounts to idiocy to presume for a moment that the Imperial Government is going to permit such flagrant violation of its traditional principles as is embraced in the measures proposed by the aforesaid ranters.

It all may be very easy to work up local sentiment sufficient to enact any legislation that suit the ideas of a portion of the community, but obtaining the sanction of the Imperial authority is a very different matter, since the fact could not very well be disguised that such laws were gotten up in the interests of a portion of the population of Natal to the prejudice and the detriment of another portion, and that they, therefore, constitute class legislation of a very pronounced type. The fact that those who are discriminated against were not born in a fashionable quarter of the empire, and have not a popular complexion counts for nothing, since all alike are entitled to a refuge under the protecting folds of the Union Jack.

It is, therefore, the rankest kind of nonsense and demagogism to put forth the idea that a law abiding resident domiciled here, who has acquired vested rights in property or established business, be he Indian, English or alien, can be ruthlessly uprooted and his right and means of obtaining a livelihood wrested from him without rhyme or reason. It is absurd to assume that a man's business, and his right to conduct it if it be an honourable and lawful one, is subject to the caprice of a licensing board for it is a fundamental principle that no one can be deprived of life, liberty or property without due process of law; and a law that does not apply to all classes of men and is gotten up for the benefit of some and the detriment of others is null and void, and this will continue to be so in every British country so long as the United Kingdom shall stand. How would it be likely to suit the European merchant to have to take the medicine he so glibly prescribes for the Asiatic merchant! *i.e.*, to be subject at any time to enforced retirement, and in the event of death to be unable to transmit his business by inheritance and necessitated to have it liquidated within a period of eighteen months?

It would certainly be very profitable and convenient for European merchants to have all their Asiatic competitors scooped up at public expense and deported in a bunch over the bar, as was suggested by a gentleman who is supposed to be learned in the law and is posing as a statesman. The question arises as to whether or not all this kind of tall talk and political bunkum would be indulged in, and such meetings convened if all the Indians of this country had a vote? If very suddenly by Imperial decree this should be the case it would be highly amusing to see how quickly these political bombasts would change their tune, and what agility they would display in hastily climbing down from their high perches, and with what alacrity they would proceed to change their coats. If they did not soon get a move on and shift their tactics, there would soon be some statesmen out of a job. Under these circumstances would we be likely to have a member of the Colonial Assembly openly boast of the fact that during his whole parliamentary career he has fought against the Indians? Is it a very valorous and laudable thing to fight a man who is bound and gagged, and has no means of defence? Would he continue the fight if there were more Indian votes than any other kind, or would he capitulate at once?

The Colonial Patriotic Union

sounds very well, but when its principles are considered it becomes apparent that it is calculated to do much more harm than good, as its avowed object is to wage a faction fight and create racial prejudice which will not be conducive to the general welfare of the country. One of the most important principles of civilisation is that every man is justly entitled to the product of his own labour. Yet these patriots (?) and these statesmen (?) fain would insist that a British Indian who by dint of honest industry, sobriety and economy has accumulated a sum of money and invested it in merchandise, could and should have his property virtually confiscated for the benefit of his European competitors, by summary measures of denying him the right to sell what he has bought and paid for. Such sentiments of patriotism are born of the old heresy that a coloured man has no rights that a white man is bound to respect. This kind of patriotism is radically wrong both legally and morally, and if it could be made effective it would undermine the whole structure of a civilised community.

The advocates of such erroneous principles are not patriots nor are they statesmanlike, they are dangerous demagogues pandering to the prejudices of the masses of unthinking people. They evidently have political axes to grind. They must have votes, and in order to get them they must cater to popular sentiment no matter how unconstitutional, unjust, irrational or inadvisable it may be. If it were not for the Imperial balance wheel they would fly off on a tangent and enact the most absurd and iniquitous legislation that would create civil war and ruin the country.

One of the greatest obstacles to the progress of Natal at the present time is its superabundance of demagogues and scarcity of statesmen. Those who are undertaking to run the ship of state have never learned governmental navigation, and they are all out at sea in a storm without a compass and without a rudder. Being panic stricken they confuse coincidence with causes, and are looking around for some Jonah to jettison that will tranquillise the troubled waters. They think they have found him in lo! the poor Indian and overboard he must go in order to avert dire disaster. The illusions and delusions of these pilots and patriots have their parallels in a child crying for the moon, or Don Quixote going out to find the wind mills. If they were statesmen they would not lose their heads in an emergency. They would recognise the fact that labour is the foundation of all wealth and that in this dilemma recourse to industry is the right way out. Development of the resources of the country is the only hope of future prosperity. The Indians instead of being a curse to the country, as it is erroneously alleged, are in reality one of its greatest blessings. They have been the wealth producers of the past and will continue to be so in the future if their energy is well directed by the superior intelligence of the European. It is by reason of their industrious habits that profitable agricultural industries have been established and maintained. They would keep right on working and creating national wealth for very small personal compensation while the patriots were looking on with their hands in their pockets growling at them and devising schemes for putting them out of action. The dignity of human labour should be upheld and encouraged, for every comfort and luxury of life is the direct result of somebody's labour. The true patriot is the one who contributes something to the world's wealth, and who leads an honourable and useful life, and is willing to accord to every other person the same rights and privileges that he claims for himself. No matter how exalted or how humble his sphere of life may be he believes in giving to his fellow-men the best products of his hand or his brain.

If they were patriots and statesmen they would not descend to the ignoble principle of stirring up strife and discord, creating racial hatred, and inciting to faction fighting, but would be induced with a desire to harmonise the whole body politic, and inculcate higher, grander, and more philanthropic sentiments that would tend to enlighten and exalt the whole commonwealth. In the industrial field there is room for every arm, and in the intellectual arena there is room for every thought. If they were patriots and statesmen their mental vision would be bright enough and their intellectual horizon would be broad enough to see that free labour will give us wealth, free thought will give us knowledge, free competition will give us energy, free speech will give us truth, and freedom of action will give us the utmost liberty to do anything and everything that does not infringe upon the rights and liberties of our fellow-men. The fact is they are not statesmen nor are they patriots, and "you can't make a silk purse out of a sow's ear." A true patriot is a lover of truth and liberty for himself and everybody else. He considers not his own selfish interests, but the interests of all; he believes in the universal brotherhood of man; he adheres to the broad sound political principle of the greatest good to the greatest number, and is guided by the greatest and most sublime moral principles recognised by the world's sages, thinkers and philosophers throughout all historic times, treasured and taught as the ne-plus-ultra of all the golden rules of conduct.

> "As ye would that others should do unto you,
> Do ye also unto them."

REMEDIAL MEASURES

are what people naturally interest themselves the most in when things are awry. It is generally admitted in all quarters that the present state of financial, political, commercial, and social affairs of the country are in a very undesirable condition, and that something needs to be done to improve matters. In a proper representative government of the people, by the people, for the people, there is no reason why they should not have just what they want and whatever is desirable to have, in so far as they are able to obtain it. The fact that we are living under and governed by an oligarchy has become a public scandal, and so long as this state of affairs is allowed to exist there will be dangers and difficulties too numerous to mention. It is essential to good government that there should be proper and adequate representation. A privileged few trying to boss up the many is like the tail endeavouring to wag the dog. It is for the purpose of curing this kind of anomaly that the redistribution movement has come to the front with the indignation that it righteously and justly deserves. The justice of its claims should be recognised and upheld. This would bring us back to the fundamental principle that "All just powers of government are derived from the consent of the governed." The right of suffrage should be based upon an intellectual qualification irrespective of sex, race or nationality. There is nothing more tyrannical or inimical to the spirit and interests of the age in which we live than compelling people to conform to laws they have had no voice in making. In a new country like this there is no reason why it should be hampered by old customs and traditions which hinder and restrain progress in old settled countries. It should aim to adopt the latest and best methods in vogue in the most enlightened and progressive countries of the world. All law abiding citizens of a certain intellectual standard have a moral right, and they should have a legal right to exercise their will in all important matters of state. A denial of this is not, in my opinion, at all conducive to the development and welfare of the country. To deprive any class of respectable and intelligent citizens of their just rights is a manifest injustice which the state cannot afford to engage in without suffering the consequences which are inevitably entailed by it. No individual can halfway succeed in life whose principles are unsound or unjust, nor can a country succeed one bit better because the same law of retribution applies equally to both. The state should aim at the highest possible development of the personality and individuality of its citizens, and the best way of promoting that is to impose upon them the full responsibilities of citizenship. It is a natural law that a fountain cannot rise higher than its source. It is, therefore, folly for a country like this to expect a legislative body to be much wiser and better than its constituency. This being the case, it is obvious that the whole matter of government is resolved right down to the point of individual responsibility; and in order to conduct an ideal system of government, the ideals of each and every citizen must of necessity be high and there must exist a disposition and an earnest endeavour to discharge their respective duties to the state to the best of their ability.

I know of no one thing that would do more towards enhancing the prosperity and general welfare of the country, if it should be adopted and strictly adhered to, than the principle expressed in the word

Justice,

which was not overrated or overdrawn by a notable jurist of New Jersey (Judge Alton B. Parker), when in response to a toast "The Importance of the Judiciary in our System of Government" expressed this sentiment:— "Justice is the greatest interest of man on earth. It is the ligament which binds civilised beings and civilised nations together. Wherever her temple stands, and so long as it is duly honoured, there is a foundation for general security, general happiness and the progress of our race." It is the disregard of this principle that constitutes the underlying cause of pretty much all the trouble existing here to-day. The adverse economic conditions have been very largely brought about by the few who have not only tried to exploit the many but have succeeded remarkably well. It is conspicuous in the question of unequal representation, of unequal taxation, the Native rebellion, and the anti-Asiatic agitation. It is safe to assert that at the bottom of almost every serious political disturbance in the way of Native revolts, Indian wars, Race riots, etc., there is lurking somewhere some kind of injustice on the part of the white man. He who inflicts upon another an act of injustice places a dangerous weapon in the hand of the one he thus injures, for there is compensation in all things. It is a political heresy that liberty and enlightenment are dangerous. We only have to look to Russia to see the baneful effects of an autocratic and unjust government.

There is, in my opinion, no safer, surer and better solution of the Native question than a policy of absolute justice to the Kafirs. They should be encouraged and assisted in everything that tends towards their mental, moral and social improvement. In consideration of their undeveloped condition they are justly entitled to education and protection. They need careful guardianship from illicit liquor sellers, avaricious money lenders, incompetent judges and prejudiced and biassed juries. Such travesties of justice as indicated in the Richmond affair, in which an innocent kafir boy was ruthlessly mutilated by a gang of white toughs who call themselves gentlemen and were exonerated by a purblind jury, is a reproach to the country;[3] and such occurances should be rendered impossible by the abolition of the jury system in such cases. If the circumstances had have been reversed, and a white boy had been the victim of kafirs, what a howl there would have been and how different the verdict. The country has a character and a reputation to maintain as well as each of its citizens, and it cannot well afford such detraction from its integrity. Mr. Jellicoe's[4] withdrawal from the Dinuzulu trial[5] in disgust, and hastily returning to England is a sad commentary upon the judicial system of Natal. It will be far reaching and deplorable in its effects.

The idea is held and advocated by many people that it is very inexpedient on the part of the whites to in any way facilitate the intellectual development of the Natives, for the reason that in the event of their improved condition they would become induced with higher aspirations than that of being mere hewers of wood and drawers of water, and might become formidable competitors in lines of skilled labour. Any kind of political recognition and equable status would be attended by claims to social equality which might lead to an undesirable admixture of the races, and the supremacy of the whites would be weakened and imperilled thereby. I mention this for the purpose of condemning it and refuting it. It is the old stock argument of the defunct pro-slavery party in America. No matter how fine it all may be in theory, facts prove to the contrary. All human experience tends to demonstrate that the problem does not work out that way. Political democracy does not necessarily lead to social equality; that matter is self regulative and needs no safeguard. All this kind of sordid pessimism fades away into the air when it is confronted with statistical information. A recent publication in America, written by Wm. H. Fleming, entitled "Slavery and the Race Problem in the South" sets forth these very significant facts:—"Considering the numerical relation of the races, the census of 1900 shows the rate of increase of the blacks in the South Atlantic States was only 14.3 from 1890 to 1900, instead of 35 per cent., as reported for a previous decade, while that of the whites stood substantially at its previous record, 20 per cent. The certainty of continued white supremacy has steadily increased with each decade. The negroes are declining because their numbers are not increased by immigration, and because the death rate among negroes is abnormally high—twice as high per thousand as among the whites. It is believed an actual decrease has set in, owing largely to the ravages of consumption and certain other diseases. Professor Wilcox, of Cornell University, and Professor Smith, of Tulane University, show that in the course of time negroes will die out from inherent and natural causes. Facts show that the white people of the South can work out their racial problem on lines of justice to the negro without imperilling white supremacy."

The same principles which apply to the negroes there apply to the kafirs here. What is considered the very much vexed Indian question is also solvable on the same basis of simple justice. If it is the consensus of opinion that there is quite enough Asiatics in the country, the only right and honourable thing to be done is to shut the door and accept the situation as it is. Europeans are responsible for their presence and they are also responsible for their good or their ill treatment. Indians are easy to govern. They will stand a tremendous amount of imposition; they are used to it. The practice of bringing in indentured Indians, which is only at best a modified form of slavery, should be put a stop to, and the free Indians should be treated with far more consideration than they now receive. The fact that they are taxed out of all proportion to their ability to pay is a flagrant piece of injustice. It is bad enough with the kafir who pays tax on his dog, his hut, and his head, and has no vote or representative whatever; but with the Indian it is much worse, for beside the poll tax, he pays three pounds a year for what? That a poverty stricken Indian, with a wife and family to support, should have to pay seven pounds a year tax, while his aristocratic and wealthy employer is grumbling about the paltry pound poll tax he is subjected to is a "comedy of errors," and constitutes a good example of taxation without representation, which is defined as tyranny.

The proposition that the indenture of Indians should be made to terminate in India, that they should be brought here to work for a term of years for a mere pittance, and then with weakened energies and broken castes returned to their own country as pariahs to eke out a miserable existence for the remainder of their lives, is utterly devoid of the least semblance of justice, and would never be sanctioned by the Indian Government.

If further Asiatic immigration should be restricted, and a protective tariff measure adopted, there would be a good outlook for future prosperity. The Natives would not materially increase, they would tend more to diminish under domestic improvement. They could be civilised to extinction. The Natal-born Indians are capable of great advancement under favourable conditions. They have the necessary intellectual capacity, and all they require is opportunity. It is a mistaken policy altogether, to say nothing of the moral aspect of the question, to boycott and abuse them. Civility and courtesy are cheap enough commodities to be given away to everybody. The best crop that any country can produce is a crop of good men and women, and in order to get that there must be good conditions. There must be liberty of thought and action and due consideration of the rights of all. It is the duty of the State to give the rising generation a show. Put them in the right way by inculcating sound principles and good morals. There is no more effectual way of doing this than by the discouragement in every possible manner of the use of

Liquor and Tobacco.

It is a lamentable fact that the youth of the period no sooner leaves off sucking his mother's breast than he starts in to sucking cigarettes; he soon graduates on to a pipe that is powerful enough to arrest his intellectual development to a very great extent and permanently dwarf and stultify his mind. In many cases this folly leads on up to the still greater evil of the use of alcoholic beverages which tends to the destruction of the whole moral and physical fabric. The pernicious effects of tobacco upon the youth is a matter of importance that is not half sufficiently recognised and appreciated. It has been practically demonstrated in American colleges that the use of tobacco is a serious menace to the mind. In Yale and Harvard though the smokers are much in the majority, not one has carried off the highest honours there for years past. Smokers, all things being equal, cannot compete with non-smokers. The University of Pennsylvania has prohibited the use of tobacco on its grounds. The Japanese are astute enough to see the advantages to be derived from their avoidance of this pitfall that has ensnared Europeans, and they have made the use of tobacco by boys a misdemeanour.

Whatever may be said against the so called Arabs, it must be admitted that they are exemplary to the Europeans in the matter of temperance, which accounts very largely for their successful rivalry in business; for the tendency of temperance is towards frugality, and the use of liquor promotes prodigality. Herein lies very largely the secret of the success of one and the failure of the other, which is erroneously attributed to unfair competition. Reverse the order of things and you would soon see the European survive and the Asiatic go to the wall.

If the liquor traffic was to be left in the hands of intelligent Indians it would soon be voted out of existence. Then we would have a Utopia here well worth talking about. We would have domestic happiness, prosperity, peace and plenty. We could then afford to stop borrowing money and set about the liquidation of our debt. This would inspire confidence to foreign capital that would come in to establish industries and Natal could lift up its head among the nations of the earth. A country that depends upon grazing and the production of raw materials will remain ignorant and poor, while the country which manufactures and supplies its own wants, subjugates and utilises the forces of Nature, will become intelligent and rich. The former, with intemperance, produces only "pot-house politicians" and a populace of mediocre minds that can readily be bamboozled by them; but the latter, with temperance, produces statesmen and an intelligent populace that appreciates proper principles of government and is willing to maintain them.

The social disabilities incident to the isolated life of the farmers can very readily be obviated by inaugurating a universal system of telephones, put up and maintained at public expense, but subject to a yearly tax sufficient to pay the interest on the cost. Each family could then have unlimited service and could report to the central office any extraordinary event of the day's doings in any locality. In the early evening there could be an hour set apart and known as the telephone hour, at which all would be rung up simultaneously and told all the important news, not only of Natal, but the purport of the telegrams from other parts of the world; also the market reports and other things of interest and then if there should be a concert or an address at the Town Hall it could be switched on for them to listen to and enjoy. This would soon elicit their interest in matters above and beyond ordinary topics of conversation which are generally confined to horses, horned cattle, mealies and potatoes, and would thus tend to make rural life more enjoyable, social, intellectual and profitable.

Throughout the whole picturesque landscape there should stand public school houses, each containing a circulating library for the free use of every citizen, and holding aloft, to float in the sweet zephyrs, the Union Jack—the emblem of liberty, equality, fraternity and prosperity.

If rightful endeavours are made to work out the salvation of this country along the lines indicated, I am constrained to believe that success is assured and cannot long be delayed. Natal may yet arise like the fabled phoenix from its ashes and become one of the brightest gems of the royal diadem.

NOTES

1. William Ewart Gladstone, prominent British statesman and parliamentary reformer. A founder of the Liberal Party and Prime Minister, 1868–1874, 1880–1885, 1886, 1892–1894.
2. These figures were either incorrectly transcribed or misprinted. The correct figures are:

Hut Tax	...	...	...	...	£121,374 18 0
Dog Tax	...	...	...	...	15,509 10 0
Total	...	...	...	...	£245,267 14 7

   Colony of Natal: Report of Native Affairs Commission 1906–7. Pietermaritzburg, 1907, p. 42.
3. Lamb is referring to a case in Richmond where five whites were accused of emasculating a young African, Mtonga, who had quarrelled with his employer, a Mr Dempster. The quarrel had ended in a fight during which Dempster had been thrashed. The emasculation arose directly out of the affair. The accused were acquitted by a white jury.
4. E. G. Jellicoe KC was engaged to defend Dinuzulu in early 1908. He threw up his brief within three weeks on the grounds that the defence was being prevented from carrying out its investigations.
5. Dinuzulu, head of the Zulu royal house. Recognized by many Zulu as King but by the Natal government as Chief of the Usuthu. Although he played no active role in the 1906 disturbances, he was accused of high treason and tried by a Special Court in 1908. Despite being found guilty only of complicity, he was sentenced to four years' imprisonment and died in exile in the Transvaal in 1913.

The Lamb Lectures

✳ ✳ ✳

About Dr. Lamb's Lectures.

What is Said and Who Says It.

From the Easton Gazette, Md.

Our readers this week are again treated to chips from the pens of foreign correspondents. . . . R. H. L. again sends a letter from Ceylon, and as usual with his numerous letters of the past, is brimful of information and droll wit. His poetical flights are not the least attractive features of his pen, and if he should treat the public one day to a book, "The American Dentist Abroad." no doubt it would fill an unoccupied niche, for the many countries he has lived in and practised his profession has given him a rare experience with the human family. His descriptive powers are fine. What could be more forcible than these few lines from his letter in another column?

" The sea breeze never ceased to blow. the birds did not weary of singing sweet song, the gorgeous colors of the magnificent sunsets did not fade, and all nature with utmost energy did ever smile."

Or more true and poetical than the closing paragraph of the same letter?

A TRUE AMERICAN.

A Former Visitor to Easton in Africa.

[There resides in Durban, Africa. a gentleman who has traveled the world over and transacted business in every Continent upon the globe.

He is a native of New Jersey. graduate of a renowned institution and a writer and lecturer of marked ability.

He has visited Easton, and many persons will remember Dr. R. H. Lamb to whom this refers.

He takes up for America wherever he travels, and makes it warm for those who oppose him in argument. Some of his printed letters in foreign papers are exceedingly entertaining. and the one subjoined is clipped from the Natal Mercury, South Africa, under date of January 8th.—Editor GAZETTE.]

A NATIVE HUT. CEYLON.

What Prof. Shortlidge says:

Concordville, Pa., April 5, 1905.

On March 30th Dr. R. H. Lamb, of Palmyra, N.J., delivered his illustrated lecture on "Ceylon," before the teachers and students of Maplewood Institute, Concordville, Pa. The Lecture was very interesting and instructive and shows great research on the part of the speaker. He is very familiar with the customs of the people, having spent several years on the island.

In 1871-72 Dr. Lamb was a student in the above institute. The school register shows that he made an excellent record while here, winning the esteem and confidence of both faculty and school mates.

In recent years he has traveled throughout the world, and possesses an extensive knowledge of many lands. Do not fail to hear his lecture on Ceylon. We have arranged to have him deliver, in the near future, a companion lecture on "Japan."

JOS. SHORTLIDGE,
Principal.

Dr. Lamb's Lectures.

Comments of People and Press.

What the New Jersey Mirror says:

Before an appreciative audience at the Friends' Meeting House on Saturday evening, Dr. R. H. Lamb, formerly of Mount Holly, delivered his lecture, illustrated with stereopticon views, on the "Island of Ceylon." Dr. Lamb's talk was instructive and he impressed his hearers with the fact that there is much to be learned and of interest in the country in which he has spent four years of his life. The views shown on the canvas gave an excellent idea of the beautiful scenery of Ceylon.

What Ex-Surrogate John R. Howell says:

It gives me great pleasure to say that I enjoyed your lecture very much indeed. It was not only interesting, but still more instructive. I am sure I enlarged my education and knowledge of Ceylon in that hour, more than *all* of my *other study* of it in all my past life.

Trusting that you may go on in your good work, I remain,

Very sincerely yours,
JOHN R. HOWELL.

What County Collector Joseph Powell says:

I enjoyed your lecture very much. It was highly instructive as well as interesting, and I was able to get more knowledge from it, than I had ever known before of Ceylon and that locality.

Hoping at some future time I may witness the lecture again, I am,

Very respectfully,
JOSEPH POWELL.

What Ex-Judge B. P. Wills, of Mount Holly, says:

It has been my privilege to listen to such an interesting lecture as that you delivered on the Island of Ceylon in Mount Holly on February 11, 1905. It was interesting and instauctive from the beginning to the end. You must have spent many months of hard work in getting so complete a history of the Island and its natural advantages. The most beautiful pictures of the people and the places exhibited made one feel as though one had really visited the country. I can sincerely say it was a treat to me, and I was very sorry when your lecture and display of pictures were over.

Yours most respectively,   BENAJAH P. WILLS.

A JAPANESE PAGODA.

What the New Era, Riverton, says:

The residents of Riverton, Palmyra and vicinity who failed to attend the lecture of Dr. R. H. Lamb on Ceylon, on Wednesday evenind last, the 8th inst., at Morgan Hall, Palmyra, missed an intellectual treat. The doctor handles his subject with skill and ability. His address is most interesting and the stereopticon views are really fine. The audience was large, considering the very inclement weather. This lecture is destined to become more and more popular.

BELLAIR HYDROPATHIC INSTITUTION.

HEALTH.—*A perfect circulation of pure blood in a sound organism.*

The above Institution is established for the benefit of the people of *South Africa.* It is an ideal Health Resort for convalescents needing rest and change, and a quiet comfortable home with good nursing for the sick.

It is superbly situated on one of the Bellair Hills, surrounded by a beautiful landscape of fruit farms and fertile valleys overlooking Durban Bay.

The Institution is being well equipped for giving—
STEAM BATHS, SITZ BATHS, TONIC BATHS, SALINE BATHS, ALKALINE BATHS, SALT GLOWS, PACKS, SWEDISH MASSAGE, etc., etc.

All suffering from Rheumatism, Sciatica, Lumbago, Paralysis, Obesity, Stomach Disorder, Anaemic and Nervous Troubles should take the advantage of a short stay at this Institution.